FALKLANDS:
TASK FORCE
PORTFOLIO

HMS Hermes sails from Portsmouth - 5 April 1982.

INTRODUCTION

Many thousands of words have been written on the Falklands crisis — and no doubt there are many more to come. Rather than publish another book repeating all that we have read in the newspapers - we decided to reproduce, in this format, many of the excellent photographs that have been taken and which, we hope help record the whole massive operation.

Some of these photographs have been seen in your newspapers but we hope this book will be in circulation much longer than the average newspaper — as an historical record of the force. Other photographs, particularly those of Merchant Ships, have not been considered newsworthy for our newspapers — but the role of these humble ships was essential for the support of warships, troops and the Ascension Island base. There would be no story to tell without them.

Security and other restrictions have prevented us from using certain photographs here. We hope to publish a second book to include some of these photographs — once they are available — and to continue the story in more accurate detail of the force in the South Atlantic — to its eventual successful conclusion.

We trust that, as you look through this pictorial record of our "Magnificent Force," to quote the Prime Minister, you will at least have some insight into the operation — and perhaps be able to guess the many feelings and emotions experienced by those involved.

The men in the Ministry, factory and dockyard workers and servicemen throughout the country played as vital a role as the men — and women — who were to see "the front line" action. All played a necessary and sometimes vital part in this whole massive operation. The fact that such a force could be assembled and sail within a matter of days was, in itself, a major success story. Others seem to follow daily — although no one should think any were achieved easily.

Those who sailed with the force will have their own special memories — from hours of boredom to seconds of terror. As time passes some of these memories will fade, others never can.

From those of us who only went to war by permission of the TV cameras may we salute those who went South — or supported them by their efforts 8,000 miles away. Thank you.

Mike Critchley,
Looe,
Cornwall.

We have decided to donate a considerable proportion of any profit from the sale of this book, to the King Georges Fund for Sailors which has a magnificent record of caring for sea farers and their families over the last century — and will doubtless play a major role in caring for those on whom this operation will leave a permanent scar.

IT ALL STARTED HERE . . . 19th March 1982 . . . Argentinian Scrap-metal workers landed here on the inhospitable island of South Georgia. They had a contract to demolish a disused whaling station at Leith — but landed without British permission — and hoisted the Argentinian Flag . . . No one could ever of guessed the repercussions of this action . . .

A tiny Royal Marine detachment is rushed to South Georgia by HMS ENDURANCE. The Argentinians overrun the island and, after inflicting considerable damage to a corvette and helicopter the Royal Marines are ejected -taken to the mainland - and eventually returned home.

The Falkland Islands are invaded . . . The tiny force of Royal Marines in the Falklands are overrun and rounded up after a spirited defence of Port Stanley. They, and a team of Naval surveyors trapped on the islands - are returned to the United Kingdom.

The marines are stripped of their equipment.

And are made to lie face down in the road as the invaders move in . . .

The Falkland Islanders soon have to get used to carrying out their daily chores under the watchful eye of the invaders-who arrived in massive numbers and very well equipped.

Extensive diplomatic moves are made to solve the crisis. The United Nations condemn the Argentinian action and call for troops to be withdrawn. From the Ministry of Defence, Dockyards, Stores Depots, Shore establishments, Naval Air Stations, Civilian defence contractors a massive exercise swings into operation to assemble, provision, arm and sail a task force . . . hundreds of men are on the move around the country to join new ships and aircraft squadrons.

Nuclear Submarines are sailed - at full speed for the South Atlantic -8,000 miles from home waters . . .
HMS CONQUEROR

To get the force south a fleet of replenishment tankers of the Royal Fleet Auxiliary have to sail ahead of the warships.

One of the first — RFA Olmeda — sails from Plymouth on 5th April having embarked stores and Sea King Helicopters.

Ships programmes change by the hour . . . Here the Royal Fleet Auxiliary Landing ship SIR GERAINT loads with a wide range of Royal Marines equipment at Devonport.

At the Royal Naval Air Station, Lee-on-Solent — more aircraft than they have seen for years . . . Sea King helicopters assemble before flying to join HM Ships INVINCIBLE and HERMES in Portsmouth Dockyard.

Off Gibraltar the annual exercise SPRINGTRAIN is interrupted. Tankers and Stores ships head south instead of home. Many long hours are sent transfering practice ammunition to the store ships and re-embarking war stocks. Fuel tanks are topped up . . .

AT GIBRALTAR

The cruise liner UGANDA is taken over on the high seas. First stop is Naples where School children are landed — then its Gibraltar for a quick conversion to a hospital ship. Men and women of the medical services (from the RN Hospitals at Haslar and Stonehouse) fly out to join her.

HMS AMBUSCADE sails — they thought for Exercise Springtrain — but events were to prove otherwise.

Local dockyard workers — with the news of the Dockyard closing only recently announced — work to produce an "instant" hospital ship — and medical staff arrive onboard to convert dormitories into wards.

UGANDA sails in her new colours.

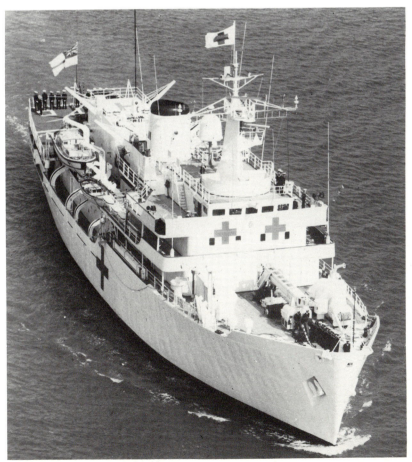

HMS HYDRA too

WARSHIPS OF THE TASK FORCE
THE FIRST SHIPS TO HEAD SOUTH

HMS GLASGOW

Ships sail south and are prepared for action - all unnecessary gear is stowed away or even thrown overboard.

HMS ANTRIM Flagship of Admiral Woodward until HMS Hermes joined the force.

HMS SHEFFIELD

Some ships were heading north after a deployment to the Gulf that started before Christmas — they soon had to reverse course. . .

HMS COVENTRY

THE OLD

The Type 12 Frigate HMS PLYMOUTH.

AND THE NEW. . . .

HMS BROADSWORD - one of the Navy's largest and most modern frigates sailed from Gibraltar.

HMS YARMOUTH — one of the Navy's oldest ships — soon to be doing the same job as ships 20 years younger.

RFA TIDEPOOL — Sold to the Chilean Navy as a defence economy, was on passage to Chile with a joint UK/Chilean crew when the crisis broke. The Chileans were landed in South America - new crew members joined -and the TIDEPOOL sailed for more, unexpected service, with the RFA. She was soon back in action pumping tons of fuel into the Task Force ships as they moved south.

HMS ARROW

HMS ANTELOPE

HMS BRILLIANT

HMS GLAMORGAN

HMS ALACRITY

AT PORTSMOUTH

After frantic activity, the Aircraft carriers HERMES and INVINCIBLE were ready to sail. Men were on leave, machinery removed for maintenance and repair but within a weekend all were in situ and the largest warships sailed out of Portsmouth — It seemed most of the city turned out to wish them well — millions of others watched on Television around the world.

HMS INVINCIBLE — due to be sold to the Australian Navy - passes Round Tower at Old Portsmouth — What a send off!

Past the War Memorial at Southsea. And so the long haul south begins . . . Aircraft have to be embarked in the Channel — no one knows what future days will bring. HRH Prince Andrew is one of the ships helicopter pilots in 820 squadron.

Many of the men who had worked extremely long hours to get her to sea watch as the heavily laden HERMES gets underway in Portsmouth Harbour.

The support tankers follow. RFA PEARLEAF - sailed with the carriers from Portsmouth.

The eventual Flagship of the force — the aging HMS HERMES finally sails from Portsmouth — much to the relief of her engineers, who along with the Dockyard, worked to the last minute to "achieve the impossible". Men — both service and civilian had worked round the clock to load her. Every conceivable corner was packed with men and machinery.

The Assault ship HMS FEARLESS sails too. A few weeks previous she was deemed surplus to the needs of the fleet and earmarked for sale - or scrap! Suddenly she was very much back in business.

FEARLESS heads down channel - her landing craft follow.

SAXONIA

Merchant Ships start arriving at Naval Ports for conversion to their new roles. A standard communication link was vital and most ships were destined to be fitted with new radio telephones to enable them to keep in touch with the fleet - via a satellite.

A "miracle" from Portsmouth Dockyard . . . RFA STROMNESS lay idle in the yard victim of recent defence cuts — ready for sale or scrap. Within a very few days she was re-commissioned as a troop transport. Mess decks were built and the ship sailed for a new lease of life — full of Royal Marine Commandos.

LOADED. . . . AND OFF —

RFA SIR GALAHAD sailed from Devonport — it turned out to be a last farewell — in just a few weeks she was bombed and ablaze off the Falklands.

RFA ENGADINE — a frequent visitor to Falmouth — returns from a training exercise off Gibraltar, reloads and sails. Her twin flight decks were soon to be handling plenty of helicopters — but no training exercise this time.

AT DEVONPORT

Cunard's ATLANTIC CONVEYOR is brought from her lay up berth on the Mersey — and is the first merchant ship to be converted into an "instant aircraft carrier" — and stores ship.

She is soon gently eased out of Plymouth Sound — it was to be her very last voyage too.

Her sistership ATLANTIC CAUSEWAY had the same conversion at Devonport — but she was fitted with a temporary shelter, built on the forward end of her upper deck to protect aircraft and men from the wild South Atlantic winter.

LAERTES sails from Plymouth with stores for tansfer to the Royal Fleet Auxiliaries at Ascension Island.

More nuclear powered submarines sail to implement the 200 mile exclusion zone around the Falklands, declared by the United Kingdom on 8th April.

The "hunter killer" submarine SPLENDID sails for many long, lonely, weeks beneath the waves.

Her sister ship SPARTAN sails too....

It was to be a long, long patrol. But where were they ? What were they watching? The Argentinian Admirals could not send their fleet to sea all the time these capital ships of today's Navy were on the loose.

And the smallest warships join the force.

Normally found patrolling our oil and gas installations in the North Sea — or on Fishery Protection duties, HMS DUMBARTON CASTLE sails from Portsmouth. Her sister ship LEEDS CASTLE sailed too. . .

Royal Marines. . .

To the South Atlantic, quick march.

Men of 42 Commando Royal Marines march off the parade ground of their camp at Bickleigh near Plymouth. Men of 40 and 45 Commando make rapid preparations — and are off too.

A quick goodbye to the family . . . and then off — by bus — to Southampton and the liner Canberra.

AT ROSYTH

The 11th Minecountermeasures Squadron is born. 5 trawlers are commissioned as HM Ships — 4 for use as minesweepers — and a support ship.

"Instant" commissioning ceremonies are held — in working gear on the jetty — but the loading must go on . . .

The commissioning cake didn't quite turn out as the chef expected so a quick trip to the shops was required to solve the problem. . .

Minesweeping gear is embarked.

HMS NORTHELLA — the latest look in minesweepers.

HMS FARNELLA — the trawl gear could be adapted to sweep mines — in stead of fish — in deep water.

Everyone knows the Bridge. . .but perhaps not the latest HM Ships as they sail to Portland to "work up".

The Royal Naval Air Station Culdrose — at least they had a proper cake. . .

A NEW SQUADRON IS BORN
AEM (R) David Duerdon, Mrs Jackie Clarke and Lt Cdr Hugh Clark cutting the cake at the Commissioning ceremony of 825 Squadron.

CULDROSE goes to war. . .

During the first weekend of April, 820 and 826 Squadrons were recalled from leave and, amidst a frenzy of activity, joined INVINCIBLE and HERMES at Portsmouth. Leave and holidays booked were soon forgotten. As aircrew, aircraft and maintainers converged on Portsmouth, Culdrose began the huge logistics exercise needed to keep upstream of the ever increasing requirements. As the Fleet sailed, Sea Kings from 706 squadron and RAF Chinooks from Odiham assisted with the heavier stores and provided a continuous helicopter delivery service to and from the ships until they were out of range in the Atlantic. In the initial exodus from Culdrose about 350 personnel disappeared — during the ensuing weeks, remaining aircraft and manpower were continually seconded to meet the increasing support requirements. 824 A Flight after 2 days back at base hurriedly departed again in RFA OLMEDA, F Flight diverted from Gibraltar in FORT AUSTIN and C and G Flight after several weeks of preparation embarked in FORT GRANGE. 771-the Search & Rescue Squadron-in the meantime lost virtually all their aircraft to Portland and the Operational Flying Training Unit of 706 Squadron broke away and formed a completely new — ten aircraft — Squadron -825-under the command of Lt Cdr Hugh Clark. The role of the new Squadron was to be that of "utility and support". They celebrated their commissioning with a service and address by Captain Jim Flindell CSO (Air) to FONAC, who spoke of their famous Squadron — 825 — being renowned for it's attacks on the Scharnhorst and Gneisenau in 1942. The then Commanding Officer — Lt Cdr Esmonde was posthumostly awarded the VC. The new "825" embarked in Atlantic Causeway at the beginning of May with a detachment of two aircraft in the QE2. With very few aircraft remaining at Culdrose by this time, the RAF temporarily took on the day and night search and rescue commitment and established 202 Squadron RAF Detachment at Culdrose operating their own Sea King aircraft.

By mid May just under 1000 people had left Culdrose for the Falklands and whatever lay ahead. News from 820 and 826 was steadily trickling back. Their work up periods during the journey South had proved strenuous but enormously rewarding -morale was high. The crossing the line ceremony was honoured in the traditional way in both ships and after the great reshuffle of stores and equipment at Ascension Island both squadrons sailed on in a high state of readiness — well practised in any number of skills that do not normally come into prominence in an Anti-submarine squadron. For 820 however, who had been in Narvic only weeks before, the prospect of deteriorating weather — from Arctic to Antarctic in less than two months could only have been rather demoralising!

Culdrose helicopters — normally seen off Cornwall in a Search and Rescue role fly off for the widest range of new missions with the force.

AT YEOVILTON TOO.

It's a 24 hour day. Sea Harriers are brought forward for front line service from training squadrons. RAF Harriers arrive for a "quick naval aquaint" before flying to join their new "Floating Airfields".

More Squadrons are born — at Yeovilton
    6th April -   809 Sea Harrier Squadron commissioned
    19th Arpil - 848 Wessex Squadron commissioned
    7th May -   847 Wessex Squadron commissioned

AIRCRAFT FOR THE FORCE

In addition to the larger Sea King and Harrier Aircraft, The Navy's "Old Faithful" the WESSEX MK5 would soon be in action. . .

and missiles from HMS ENDURANCE'S WASP were to cripple a submarine at South Georgia . . .

the more modern LYNX aircraft were to see successful action — with Sea Skua missiles for the first time . . .

and the Royal Marine Gazelle helicopters — well wrapped up for the long voyage south would soon be flying difficult and dangerous missions.

AT PORTLAND

Naval ships condense a normal work up into just a few days. . .

The assault ship INTREPID sails South — only weeks before, she too lay idle in Portsmouth Dockyard paid off as a defence economy and de-stored, ready for sale or scrap. Suddenly she is required again and in an incredibly short time is activated, stored, fueled — and at sea.

Her landing craft join - in their new colours - for docking onboard.

Cross channel ferries arrive to take on stores, helicopters and men.

EUROPIC FERRY

The BP Tanker BRITISH ESK is fitted with replenishment at sea equipment before heading south. Within a few weeks British Esk — designed for a crew of 40 — had to accommodate an incredible total of 311 men for the 15 day voyage from the Falklands back to Ascension. Most of the extra men were suriviors from HMS SHEFFIELD.

And the trawlers head South for possible use around the Falklands - the Argentinians say they have mined local waters.

AT CHATHAM

With the Naval Base destined to close in 1984 many facilities are already being run down. However stores are despatched to the fleet — and ships in the standby squadron are brought forward.

Here HMS FALMOUTH sails for a new lease of life — she and her sister ships were reprieved from the sales and scrap list and brought forward for service in the sadly depleted fleet in Home Waters and NATO area.

Other ships brought out of Mothballs at Chatham included the frigates BERWICK and ZULU — while GURKHA and TARTAR were towed to Rosyth and Devonport respectively, for refit — and further service.

Pride of the P & O Fleet — The liner CANBERRA is taken over. Helicopter landing pads are built — almost overnight.

Stores, no longer needed for cruising, are landed and military equipment loaded.

A constant stream of men . . .

and stores are loaded round the clock.

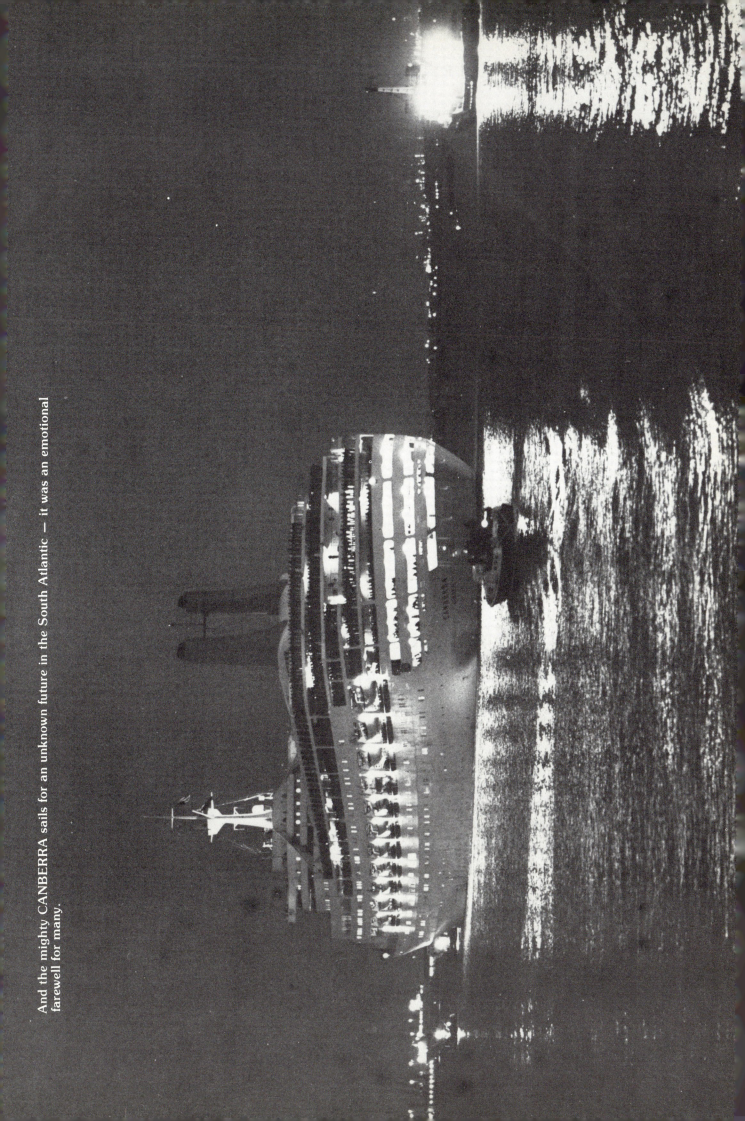

And the mighty CANBERRA sails for an unknown future in the South Atlantic — it was an emotional farewell for many.

As she heads down channel, helicopters from 706 squadron at Culdrose fly out yet more and more stores.

The Destroyer HMS EXETER — on duty as guardship in the West Indies — is diverted to join the force.

Familiar ships in an unfamiliar role.

Three of the Navy's Ocean Survey ships HECLA, HYDRA and (here) HERALD are pressed into service as 'Ambulance ships' — destined to carry the injured to the hospital ship UGANDA and hospitals ashore.

Ships of the Royal Maritime Auxiliary Service are soon sent south to stand by for duty with the force.

The Ocean going Tug TYPHOON.

And the Boom Defence Vessel GOOSANDER.

RMAS ADEPT

In home waters, other ships of the RMAS work many long hours of overtime — ferrying stores and ammunition around the Naval Bases. Throughout the dockyards, tea breaks and demarcation disputes are forgotten — many men even forget what a good night's sleep is . . .

RMAS BEAULIEU

PORTSMOUTH

The dockyard is under threat of a major rundown as a result of the 1981 defence review. Suddenly the men — with redundancy notices in their pockets, have to cope with a massive influx of merchant ships. Most have to be adapted to Ministry requirements . . . Even the men who have worked in the yard all their lives are amazed at the results achieved in a very short space of time.

The North Sea ferry NORLAND sails in her new role of troop ship.

Replenishment at Sea equipment is installed on merchant ships so they can be fuelled and provisioned when out in the wide expanses of the South Atlantic.

THE ROYAL FLEET AUXILIARY

The majority of the Royal Fleet Auxiliary were soon in the South Atlantic — whilst merchant ships were "Taken up from trade" to bring stores south. These stores and fuel would eventually have to be transferred to the RFA's for the voyage into — or close to — the total exclusion zone.

The first RFA to head South from Gibraltar was the fleet's largest (23,000 tonnes) "floating supermarket". RFA FORT AUSTIN carries the widest range of Naval, Aircraft and Victualling stores in her massive holds.

Two of the "heavies'".

RFA TIDESPRING in addition to her tons of fuel also fulfilled a useful role as a "mini" helicopter carrier.

RFA REGENT — very much a target for the Argentine Air Force — laden with ammunition for use ashore and afloat.

Her sister ship RFA RESOURCE kept warships topped up with a constant supply of ammunition too.

RFA FORT GRANGE — soon sailed south to join her sistership.

TANKERS OLD

RFA PLUMLEAF

& TANKERS NEW

RFA BRAMBLELEAF: RFA BAYLEAF the newest ship to join the RFA service also served in the fleet.

RFA APPLELEAF — sailed away — tanks full, rather than empty, as photographed here.

RFA OLNA completed the list of tankers with the force —

All the six landing ships of the RFA service were soon in action with the Force — Two were later to be the target of a devastating Argentinian air attack.

RFA SIR LANCELOT

A calm weather photograph. In rougher weather these flat bottomed craft are extremely lively — ask anyone who went south in one.

RFA SIR BEDIVERE — Practices a beach landing.

RFA SIR TRISTRAM — weeks later she was ablaze from stem to stern after a daylight bombing raid.

RFA SIR PERCIVALE.

A rapid back up for the small RFA fleet was needed. Some of the merchant ships needed to keep the fleet supplied with vital fuel, food and spares are photographed here.

AVELONA STAR — a frequent visitor to the South Americas prepared for another trip — but in a very different role.

BRITISH TRENT

BALTIC FERRY
— soon to be in the "front line" during the initial landings on the Falklands.

NORDIC FERRY

Have spanners — will travel!

M/V STENA SEASPREAD — A sophisticated North Sea support vessel — is pressed into service as a Fleet Repair ship, which sailed with many highly skilled technicians on board.

Tugs too — it will be a long tow home if ships are damaged.
IRISHMAN

YORKSHIREMAN

Pride of the United Towing Fleet. . . SALVAGEMAN.

Normally seen carrying Bananas to this country, GEESTPORT made a suitable refridgerated cargo ship for the fleet.

At least she would be at home — The tiny ST HELENA normally plies the lonely outposts of the South Atlantic — Here at Portsmouth Dockyard she becomes a support ship for the minesweepers sent south.

MORE AND MORE TANKERS. . .
No one has calculated the tons of fuel needed to keep ships steaming, aircraft flying and the humble outboard engine turning . . . but it kept a very large number of tankers busy — transfering this vital fuel from one side of the world to the other.

VINGA POLARIS

HANS MAERSK

ESSO FAWLEY

BALDER LONDON

A superb "pilots eye view" of the latest aircraft carrier for the force.

ASTRONOMER at Devonport

BRITISH WYE

From the Swedish Merchant fleet.
CORONA

More ships join the force.

It was even longer haul for HMS CARDIFF — from Mombassa — to Gibraltar — to the Falklands some 12,000 miles.

HMS ARDENT. For her too it was to be her final voyage.

HMS MINERVA

HMS PENELOPE — for many years the trials ship for the Sea Wolf missle system. She was refitted shortly before the crisis broke with Exocet missiles and rejoined the active fleet after many years as a floating test bed.

Sea Wolf — here on the foc'sle of HMS ANDROMEDA — was later to prove itself when the Argentinian Air Force came on the scene.

THE FLEET HEADS SOUTH. . . .

Ascension Island — mid way between UK and the Falklands becomes a Military Garrison "Tented Town". RAF and Naval Aircraft virtually take over the airstrip. The Island became a forward operating base. Stores could be switched from ship to ship in calmer waters. This was the last chance to 'get it right'

The ATLANTIC CONVEYOR — one of the last photographs — laiden with Harriers, Chinook Heavy Lift Helicopters, and thousands of tons of stores. The calm waters didn't last for long.

Men of 42 Commando Royal Marines transfer from the CANBERRA to a landing craft for a days training on the Island.

More men are landed on Ascension — for the last minute rehearsal. The chance to step ashore during a long ocean passage in cramped conditions is much appreciated.

Weapons are tested on the barren landscape of the Island.

Back at sea yet more stores are moved from ship to ship — here, by the Wessex helicopter from RFA REGENT.

TV camera's start recording much of the action.

At home families of men in the force were soon to become "News addicts" as no news broadcast could be missed. Hanrahan, Fox and Nicholson — just some of the reporters with the Task Force became household names as relatives at home listened intently to their every word.

For men aboard CANBERRA — keeping in top physical condition was a high priority. This "trot round the upper deck" was a 6 mile speed march!

On board INVINCIBLE there was time for a Squadron photograph. 820 Squadron aircrew — including Prince Andrew.

Troop drills are practised — over and over again. The politicians don't seem to be making much headway despite all the talking — next time it could be for real. . . .

Everything that can be moved underneath a helicopter — is.

IN MEMORIAM

POACMN K S CASEY
846 Naval Air Squadron
Lost in a Flying Accident
April 23rd

The first casualty from the Task Force —
Sadly there were to be many more.

But still the tankers arrive at Naval ports, top up and sail. . .

ANCO CHARGER

BRITISH AVON

G.A. WALKER

The cable ship IRIS — from the Post Office — joined the fleet as a despatch vessel.

Never in the newspaper headlines — but still more and more tankers are needed to take a wide range of oil products to Ascension Island — and the string of ships spread out from UK to the Falklands.

BRITISH FERN.

BRITISH DART

The petrol companies are well represented.

From Shell — EBURNA

and Esso — ESSO MILFORD HAVEN

and B.P. . . BRITISH IVY

BRITISH TAMAR

from Sweden

CORTINA

and Finland too. SHELLTRANS

Ships other than those photographed here also saw valuable service with the Force. Photographs of

    TOR CALEDONIA
    STENA INSPECTOR
    ELK
    FINNAGER
    FORT TORONTO
    LUMINETTA
    ORIONMAN
    PICT
    BRITISH TAY
    BRITISH TEST
    WIMPEY SEAHORSE

were not available in time for publication.

ALVEGA

SCOTTISH EAGLE

BACK IN DEVONPORT

It's still more like a commercial shipyard. There's hardly a warship in sight.

Sealink joins up. The Sealink cross channel ferry ST EDMUND has two large helicopter landing platforms built - forward and aft.

As the job is nearly finished stores are embarked through the stern door. Holiday makers cars last week — dockyard trucks this . . .

Onboard the CONTENDER BEZANT hatches are covered and a flat flight deck produced. Secure points are welded in to enable aircraft to be lashed to the deck.

A huge ramp had to be constructed from the helicopter deck to storage areas below. Here four (of the 50) Rosyth dockyard workers sent to Devonport to help out, weld — and weld — and weld. 400,000 feet of welding rods were used in just a few weeks on these merchant ships at Devonport.

As the days pass more and more R.A.F. aircraft are earmarked for the Force. HERCULES and NIMROD Aircraft are converted with in flight re-fuelling equipment to enable them to operate from Ascension Island. Months of work are condensed into days as aircraft are adapted for a new role.

NIMROD submarine hunters leave their bases in Cornwall and Scotland.

MORE RE-INFORCEMENTS SAIL.

The second wave of warships sailing to join the force have all their pennant numbers and identification marks removed. Here the Guided Missle destroyer BRISTOL slips quietly out of Portsmouth Harbour.

and HMS BACCHANTE too.

HMS HERMES becomes Flagship for the Force, embarking Rear Admiral "Sandy" Woodward at sea.

Flying continues — everyone has to get it right — this is not turning out to be "yet another exercise". Argentina has submarines at sea. Sea King Aircraft must be kept airborne 24 hours a day, hunting for them. They are very small needles — in a very large haystack. The work load of the maintainance men to keep the aircraft 100% serviceable is enormous.

Sea Harriers — at the ready.

There are not many available — more are desperately needed from the UK. Pilots — both RN and RAF — are to spend many long hours in the cockpit waiting for the word to go. . .

Time is made for a little relaxation — as INVINCIBLE crosses the Equator Captain J.J. Black escorts King Neptune to hold court onboard. For the ship, and most men on board, it was their first "crossing the line".

FURTHER SOUTH. . .

The weather gets steadily worse. . .

Life onboard a small warship packed with men gets "tedious" day after day in seas like this. Then there are the Argentinian airforce and submarines to think about too. . . .

FIRST STOP. . . SOUTH GEORGIA

In abysmal weather conditions men of the "special forces" are secretly landed on the bleak island by submarine and aircraft — but the aircraft crashes — then a relief aircraft too. Eventually all the men involved are recovered safely.

The Argentinians ashore are "softened up" by Naval Gunfire — here from HMS ANTRIM.

The Argentinian Submarine SANTA FEE is caught by Naval helicopters bringing more and more men and equipment to Gritviken. They attack her and she is just able to make the harbour before finally sinking — with just a little more help from the RN.

After token resistance the Royal Marines take over again. The Argentinian surrender is signed by Lt Cdr Alfredo Astiz onboard HMS PLYMOUTH. Captain David Pentreath (R) of HMS PLYMOUTH and Captain Nicholas Barker of HMS ENDURANCE accept the surrender. Lt Cdr Astiz is eventually sent to Ascension — and UK for possible interview regarding alledged acts of international terrorism.

The Union Flag and White Ensign are hoisted once again.

Argentinian casualties from the assault are buried by the Royal Navy in the local cemetery — witnessed by their colleagues.

After the long haul South, ships of the force at last find some calm water after re-taking the Islands. . .

The Destroyer ANTRIM led the detachment from the main Task Force.

RFA TIDESPRING provided vital fuel, stores and helicopters throughout the mission.

HMS ENDURANCE — normally the only Royal Naval ship to be seen in the South Atlantic rushed a small Royal Marine detachment to South Georgia to eject the original team of scrapmen. Many long weeks were spent in the area. Here she lies at anchor (with HMS PLYMOUTH) after South Georgia is returned to British rule.

The Argentinians are rounded up.

and taken off the island for the long haul back to Ascension — and eventually home.

And the Royal Marines move in with their stores for a long lonely winter on this isolated outpost.

With South Georgia safely back in British hands the Force continues to the Falklands . . . The weather varies from good — to bad — to awful. . .

Whilst the threat of other nuclear powered submarines in the area kept the rest of the Argentine Fleet in local costal waters, the submarine HMS CONQUEROR tracked the second largest warship in the Argentine Fleet — the Cruiser GENERAL BELGRANO. She was heading round the exclusion zone — probably making for South Georgia. Her presence in the area was too great a risk for the Force Commander . . . orders were given — Sink the Belgrano.

GENERAL BELGRANO slowly sinks — her two escorting destroyers clear the area in case of a second attack. Liferafts leave the ships side — and over 700 men are saved in a huge search and rescue mission — over 300 men are however lost in the freezing southern ocean.

AIRCRAFT POUND STANLEY AIRPORT..

Ageing RAF Vulcans are reprieved from the scrapman and converted from their nuclear bombing role to conventional bombers. After some hasty training in Scotland they too head for Ascension Island. With air-to-air refuelling they can fly to and from Port Stanley. Two night raids were made on the runway by the Vulcans — and Sea Harriers.

A Sea Harrier pilot disembarks from his aircraft after a sortie from HMS INVINCIBLE. HMS HERMES is in the background.

It was later discovered that the mission had only been partially successful. Bomb craters covered only half the runway. Skilled Argentinian pilots continued to fly in and out of Port Stanley by night — avoiding the craters.

Suddenly, just 2 days after the GENERAL BELGRANO is sunk — an Exocet missile — fired from an Argentinian aircraft slams into HMS SHEFFIELD. It was seen just seconds before but by only a handful of men.

The missile — luckily — didn't explode — but the ensuing fire and smoke rapidly spread throughout the "Shiny Sheff". For hours her crew fought the blaze — but in the end there was no hope.

Helicopters from HMS HERMES, and the frigate HMS ARROW, were soon on the scene to pluck survivors to safety. 20 men died. It could easily have been many more.

"The men were quite incredible . . . I'm sure every Captain would say that his ships company were the best — but I know mine is" — Captain "Sam" Salt RN — HMS SHEFFIELD.

IN MEMORIAM. . . MAY 4th

LIEUTENANT NICHOLAS TAYLOR RN — is killed when his Sea Harrier is shot down over Goose Green Airstrip.

HMS SHEFFIELD

JOHN WOODHEAD (40) Lieut. Cdr.	**ROBERT FAGAN (34)** POCK.
DAVID BALFOUR (37) Lieut. Cdr.	**ALLAN KNOWLES (31)** LMEM(M).
RICHARD EMLY (36) Sub- Lieut.	**TONY MARSHALL (31)** LCK.
BRIAN WELSH (34) Master at Arms.	**ADRIAN WELLSTEAD (26)** LЄK.
KEVIN SULLIVAN (35) WEA1.	**DAVID OSBORNE (22)** Cook.
ANTHONY EGGINGTON (35) WEA1.	**ANDREW SWALLOW (18)** Cook.
MICHAEL TILL (35) ACWEMN.	**KEVIN WILLIAMS (20)** Cook.
BARRY WALLIS (26) WEMN2.	**NIGEL GOODALL (20)** Cook.
ANTHONY NORMAN (25) POWEM (R)	**DARRYL COPE (21)** Catering Assistant
DAVID BRIGGS (25) POMEM(M).	**LAI CHI KEUNG (31)** Laundryman.

MAY 6th

LT CDR JOHN EYTON — JONES RN and LT WILLIAM CURTIS RN Lost whilst flying Sea Harriers in poor weather conditions — a mid air collision is considered the probable cause.

The price that had to be paid. Ships can be replaced — but never the men.

BUT BACK AT HOME. . . .

Pride of the Merchant Navy — the Queen Elizabeth 2nd joins the long list of ships pressed into service. .
Helicopter landing pads are installed.

Men of the Gurkhas, Welsh and Scots Guards arrive onboard.

And the ship sails from Southampton for a quick passage with the re-inforcement troops. Her destination
was South Georgia where men could be transfered to the assault ships in calm water.

The World's most Luxurious Liner has never had passengers like this.

A gun salute from HMS LONDONDERRY (herself saved from the scrapyard by the crisis) as she sails past the Dorset Coast.

the preparations still go on. . .

M/V RANGATIRA at Plymouth. A former ferry brought from layup at Falmouth — after service as a floating hotel for oil workers in Shetland. She headed for Southampton to embark more troops — and nurses.

Shipbuilders pull out the stops to advance the delivery of new warships. HMS LIVERPOOL is completed well ahead of schedule at Birkenhead and HMS BRAZEN on the Clyde. HMS ILLUSTRIOUS (below) sails from her builders on the Tyne — 3 months early. Her ships company expect their orders to head South too . . .

STRATHEWE heads South — her deck cargo includes the ramped landing craft ANTWERP and ARRAMANCHES.

CEDARBANK too — her decks full to capacity with heavy military equipment.

ONE SHIP GOES TO WAR.....

HMS GLASGOW left the UK on 8 March for two weeks of trials en route to the Gibraltar Exercise Areas. She expected to take part in Exercise SPRINGTRAIN, one of the UK's major annual maritime exercises, before returning in early April for a Families 'day at sea' and a period of well earned leave. . . That was the plan — but . . .

ON APRIL FOOLS DAY.....

The ship was working defence watches for the exercise which had been fairly quiet until then. That evening the RN Ships were conducting a night encounter exercise with the Portugese Navy. All ships were darkened, radar and radio silent and ships were zig-zagging at high speed. It was during the middlewatch on the morning of 2 April that "the signal" arrived, just as contact was made with the 'enemy for tonight' — the Portugese frigates and fast patrol boats. It took just a few minutes to stop the exercise and order the group of warships to form up-and turn South. By now men on watch knew what was happening and would pass the news to their reliefs at 4 a.m. The whole 'war preparations' organisation swung into action. At breakfast the Captain addressed the ships company to keep everybody fully informed. As the Americans would say "This is no drill". Exercise SPRINGTRAIN was suddenly over.

THE LONG HAUL SOUTH

As the ships from the exercise assembled, some had to be sent back to the United Kingdom. Those heading North transferred extra food, ammunition, stores and personnel to the southbound ships in order to increase their ability to work without Royal Fleet Auxilliary Support ships for as long as possible. Each southbound ship paired with a northbound ship to exchange stores as required. With little warning the largest simultaneous RAS (Replenishment at Sea) for a long time took place with remarkable smoothness. Helicopters transferred stores and ammunition aft to the flightdeck whilst food and personnel came across on jackstays forward. GLASGOW'S 'twin' was HMS DIDO whose ships company almost emptied their stores rooms in order to help. She also took hastily written letters and telegrams to families back home. The planned Families day was forgotten by the men at sea — but not by small children at home.

After the transfer, ships headed South. Plans were made for a controlled change into a war state. Internal and external exercises increased in complexity. Amongst the changes made between heading South and entering the Total Exclusion Zone (TEZ) were:-

Issuing survival suits and carrying life jackets at all times.

Wearing "Dog Tags" and carrying Geneva Convention Identity cards.

Sleeping in clothes.

Preparing all weapons to a 'ready at moments notice' state, i.e. loaded and ready to go.

All practice gear stowed or transferred to homegoing ships'

Noticeboards, Pictures and Trophies packed securely away.

After a brief stop out of sight of Ascension Island GLASGOW continued South. By now in defence watches, 12 hours a day 'on watch', 12 hours a day 'on call' for Action Stations. By the last week of April the Destroyer was waiting for the Carrier Group just outside the TEZ. At any moment a signal was expected enabling the ship to be 'sent in' to enforce the area. That signal arrived on the 26th April, when the carriers arrived. More exercises followed as she assumed her new role as an Air Defence Ship — about 20 miles away from the carriers and towards the Argentinian air bases. "The job" was to act as a radar picket providing early warning of an air attack, to control Sea Harriers ahead of the ship and provide a missile barrier against any aircraft the Combat Air Patrol Harriers missed.

FIRST SHIPS IN THE TEZ

HMS GLASGOW entered the TEZ on the First of May, the first British surface ship to do so since the Falklands had been invaded a month before. That day proved to be very busy as a major air attack was launched against the Task Force. The Combat Air Patrol Harriers had a busy day - with GLASGOW out in front.

SKUA GAINS ITS SPURS

At an early stage of the Falklands crisis Sea Skua fitted Lynx helicopters had been flown out to the force. These air to surface missiles were to be used with great success early in the confrontation. On the day the GENERAL BELGRANO was sunk by torpedo, GLASGOW's Lynx and one other were scrambled from the Task Force when two Argentinian patrol vessels were found to the North of the Islands, well inside the TEZ. The first Lynx scored a first time hit on one of the ships with Sea Skua. HMS GLASGOW's Lynx was then ordered to search for survivors. As it made its search the Argentinian ship opened fire! After pulling clear of the line of fire the Lynx went into an attack — severely damaging the second ship. Sea Skua had been proved on its first outing.

HMS SHEFFIELD

When the Exocet hit HMS SHEFFIELD she was in the adjacent picket station. HMS GLASGOW was thus the closest ship to her and started to move in to provide assistance. It was soon decided that this move should be abandoned — and GLASGOW remain on air picket — in case of further attacks. Other ships from the main body provided assistance to the burning ship. On board the feeling was very much "There, but for the Grace of God go I". Nearly all onboard knew somebody from the "SHINY SHEFF".

FIRST SEA KING ON A TYPE 42

A few days later GLASGOW received a message that a Sea King carrying survivors from the Argentinian Spy Ship 'NARWHAL' was running short of fuel whilst attempting a long range SAR mission. HMS GLASGOW was asked to provide Helicopter In Flight Refueling. Unfortunately the Sea King's gear was unserviceable. Rapid preparations were made for it to land on the flightdeck. It was going to be very tight and the first time such a large helicopter had ever landed on the relatively small deck of a Type 42 destroyer. Eventually it landed on safely, refuelled and made it back to its own ship. The sight of the "miniature Glasgow airport" must have been a great relief to the Sea King pilot — and his passengers!

NEWS FROM HOME

Now and again mail arrived from the UK. This event was eagerly awaited by everybody. Thoughts were of families at home. Were they allright? What were they reading in the papers? Of the many letters and messages received, a simple "Gods Blessing" from the Children of Wards 7A and 7B in the Royal Hospital for Sick Children in Glasgow, the ship's adopted charity, was much appreciated.

THE STORY SO FAR — A SOUTH ATLANTIC DIARY

March 19 — Scrap-metal workers, hired to dismantle a disused whaling station, land without British consent at Leith, South Georgia and hoist the Argentine flag.

April 2 — Argentine troops invade the Falklands Islands from the sea.

Massive operations start to prepare the Task Force.

April 4 — United Nations condemns Argentine aggression and calls for withdrawal of troops. South Georgia falls after fierce battle with the small Royal Marines contingent.

April 5 — Lord Carrington resigns as Foreign Secretary. First ships in Britains task force sail.

April 6 — U.S. Secretary of State, Alexander Haig, starts peace-seeking mission. Mr. Francis Pym appointed Foreign Secretary.

April 8 — Britain declares a 200 mile exclusion zone around Falklands with effect from April 12. Argentine Junta responds with its own South Atlantic operations zone.

April 9 — P & O liner Canberra sails from Southampton for the war zone.

April 16 — Task force sails from Ascension Island after brief stop-over, for the South Atlantic.

April 21 — First contact between Task Force and Argentinians — Royal Navy Sea Harrier intercepts and warns off Boeing 707 "Snooping" over the Force.

April 22 — Two helicopters crash on South Georgia as SBS unit is put ashore. No casualties.

April 25 — South Georgia recaptured with no British casualties. M. Company 42 Commando RM first ashore as Major Guy Sheridan leads two hour operation. Argentine submarine Santa Fe crippled. About 190 prisoners are taken.

April 26 — Lt Cdr Alfredo Astiz signs document of surrender of South Georgia.

April 28 — Blockade around Falklands extended by Britain to exclude aircraft of all nations as well as ships.

April 30 — Argentina declares 200-mile "no-go" zone covering same area as Britain's total exclusion zone.

May 1 — Haig peace mission ends in failure. United States at last decides to join EEC countries to back Britain with economic sanctions — and offers military supplies.

Sea Harriers shoot down one Mirage fighter and one Canberra bomber. Second Mirage accidentally shot down by Argentine aircraft. HMS Arrow slightly damaged. RAF Vulcan bomber craters Port Stanley airfield, Sea Harriers follow up with bomb and rocket attacks around Port Stanley and Goose Green airstrips.

Cunards flagship, Queen Elizabeth 2 is requisitioned as a troop carrier.

May 2 — Argentine cruiser, the General Belgrano, sunk by torpedoes fired by H.M.S. Conqueror 36 miles outside the "total exclusion" zone.

May 3 — Lynx helicopters attack two Somoto-class tug gun boats with Sea Skua missiles after the vessels had fired on Sea Kings from HMS Hermes. Comodoro Somellera is sunk and Alferez badly damaged.

May 4 — Lieut. Nicholas Taylor RN is killed when his Sea Harrier is shot down during attack on Goose Green airfield. RAF Vulcan again bombs Port Stanley runway.

H.M.S. Sheffield, is hit by an Exocet missile fired by an Argentine aircraft. 20 men died, 24 injured.

May 6 — Contact lost with two Sea Harriers. Pilots Lieut. Cdr. John Eyton-Jones and Lieut. William Curtis missing presumed dead. Peace efforts led by Peru end in failure.

May 7 — Britain widens war zone to within 12 nautical miles of Argentina's coast. New peace initiative is launched by United Nations Secretary-General, Javier Perez de Cuellar.

May 9 — Narwal, an Argentine fishing vessel said to have been used as spy ship, is strafed by two Royal Navy Sea Harriers. One member of the crew is killed and 13 injured. Narwal boarded but later sinks. An Argentine helicopter is shot down by a missile from a British warship. Army Garrison around Port Stanley bombarded by British warships.

May 10 — Argentine supply ship shelled and blown up by HMS Alacrity operating for first time inside the Falkland Sound between the two main islands. H.M.S. Sheffield sinks while under tow to safe anchorage in South Georgia.

May 11 — Argentinian Puma helicopter shot down. Warships bombard Port Stanley troop installations again.

May 12 — Queen Elizabeth 2 sails from Southampton for the war zone. Four Argentine Sky Hawk fighter bombers escorting flights into the Falklands are shot down. Argentine aircraft holes a British destroyer with a bomb which does not explode.

The days that lie ahead. . . .

Sea Wolf away. . . .

And Sea Cat too. . .

ASHORE IN THE FALKLANDS . . .

South Georgia is re-taken — Argentina refuses to pull her invasion troops from the Falklands — the diplomats fail to find any solution — so the main invasion plans are swung into effect . . .

Major General Jeremy Moore holds up the surrender document at Port Stanley. But so much happened between these two photographs being taken . . .

There was still a great deal of photographic material arriving from the South Atlantic as this book was published. A second part is being prepared which will complete the story of this fantastic operation. Write if you wish to be informed of the publication date.

MARITIME BOOKS: DULOE : LISKEARD : CORNWALL : U.K.